MW00952969

Name:....................................
Email:....................................
Phone:....................................

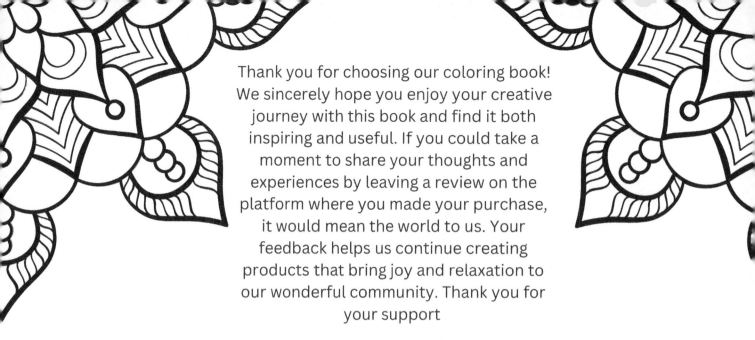

Thank you for choosing our coloring book!
We sincerely hope you enjoy your creative
journey with this book and find it both
inspiring and useful. If you could take a
moment to share your thoughts and
experiences by leaving a review on the
platform where you made your purchase,
it would mean the world to us. Your
feedback helps us continue creating
products that bring joy and relaxation to
our wonderful community. Thank you for
your support

Follow the link or QR code
for freebies and to discover
our latest books.
https://linktr.ee/qdix

Please tear out this page and place it behind the Page you are coloring to reduce the chance of colors going through to the image on the following page.

FAQs

Can I photocopy the pages for multiple uses?

Yes, photocopying this material, including pages from Qdix Press coloring books, is allowed for personal use or use in an educational institution. This coloring book is protected by copyright, and making copies to sell/distribute, infringes on the artist's rights. If you want multiple copies, consider purchasing additional books or looking for digital versions on www.qdix/etsy.com

Can I frame and display my colored pages?

Absolutely! Once you've completed coloring a page, you can frame and display it like any other piece of art. Many coloring enthusiasts choose to showcase their finished works as they can turn out incredibly beautiful and sophisticated. Feel free to also post your finished works on https://www.instagram.com/qdixcolor

How do I avoid smudging when coloring with markers?

To prevent smudging, it's essential to work from top to bottom or from left to right if you're left-handed. Place a scrap sheet of paper under your hand to avoid direct contact with the grayscale image. Additionally, allow enough drying time for the markers before moving to another section.

Welcome to QDIX Press Books

Whether you're new to coloring or just getting started, we're here to guide you on your coloring journey. Our coloring books are designed with beginners in mind, and we want to ensure you have an enjoyable and fulfilling experience.

Here are some tips and tricks to help you make the most of your coloring adventure:

1. Specialty Effects: Consider adding some special effects to your coloring, such as metallic or glitter gel pens, watercolor pencils, or pastel chalks. These can add a touch of shimmer, texture, or softness to your artwork.
2. Color Selection: Don't be afraid to experiment with colors!
3. Layering and Blending: If you want to add depth and dimension to your coloring, try layering and blending different colors. Start with lighter shades and gradually build up to darker tones.
4. Practice Different Techniques: Explore various coloring techniques, such as shading, hatching, or stippling. Play with different strokes and textures to bring your artwork to life.
5. Protect Your Pages: Consider using a spare sheet of paper to prevent colors bleeding through the pages and protect the following artwork.
6. High-Quality Coloring Mediums: Invest in good-quality colored pencils, markers, or gel pens. They offer vibrant pigments, smooth application, and better blending capabilities, allowing you to achieve stunning color effects.
7. Embrace Imperfections: Remember, there are no right or wrong ways to color. Embrace any imperfections or "mistakes" as unique and part of your artistic expression.
8. Enjoy the Journey: Above all, enjoy the process of coloring! Let it be a joyful and meditative experience that allows you to express yourself and find inner peace.

We hope these tips and tricks help you embark on a wonderful coloring adventure. Remember, the most important thing is to have fun and let your creativity shine through!

Happy coloring!

Made in the USA
Las Vegas, NV
28 December 2024

15312476R10059